DOWNTOWN UP

Photography by Sandy Bleifer

DOWNTOWN UP

Copyright © 2014-2019 by Sandy Bleifer.
All rights reserved. No part of this book may be reproduced in any manner without written permission except in the case of brief quotations included in critical articles and reviews. For information, please contact the author at sandy@sandybleifer.com

ISBN: 978-1-7330719-0-1
Library of Congress Control Number: 2019907981

DOWNTOWN UP
A photographic narrative of the return to economic and social viability of downtown Los Angeles, which began in the mid-1990s. The pictures simulate a focused walk through the Historic Core - its rich architectural detail, its human-scaled density and its reconnection to the modern office towers on Bunker Hill - looping back to the Central Business District and graphically illustrating how the built environment - both old and new - made the present revitalization possible.

Photography: Sandy Bleifer
Book Design by MicheleCastagnetti / AcrylicAirlines.com

Published by Sandy Bleifer / Bleifer InPrint

www.sandybleifer.com

DOWNTOWN UP

Downtown Los Angeles has been late to realize its potential as the centerpiece of a great American city because, at a critical juncture when LA looked forward, it opted to suburbanize and left behind its older properties and neighborhoods. Future-focused developers did not think we needed history or nostalgia as they continued to expand their frontier mentality. Like Toronto, St. Louis and many other cities, LA chose to disregard their urban center and invent new neighborhoods. The only thing left to do downtown was to raze the old mansions on Bunker Hill that had become slum housing as the wealthy moved West and build office tower/islands for professionals serving the government center around City Hall.

The development of the high-rise office towers on Bunker Hill in the seventies cast a shadow on the historic core at the bottom of the hill. Throughout the eighties a magnificent heritage of twenties-era Beaux Arts, Spanish Revival and Art Deco office buildings, department stores and theaters languished. Then, in the nineties a handful of visionaries dreamed new uses for outdated buildings. The great irony in the successful redevelopment of Downtown Los Angeles has been that the very area which was abandoned in the late nineteen seventies, the Historic Core, now is revealed to be the source of its greatest prosperity.

This photo essay shows why that happened: The photographs look up from the street level to spotlight the extraordinary beauty and inherent potential of the buildings despite boarded storefront windows and the empty spaces behind the grime and neglect. The sequence of these photographs take you on a walking tour from the Historic Core, up Angel's Flight to Bunker Hill and down the Bunker Hill Steps to the Central Business District following the evolving relationship between the revitalization of the Historic Core and its growing connectivity to Bunker Hill. Public Art and great architecture draw you along. The journey creates a narrative drawn from an inventory of architectural and cultural assets captured at a turning point in the mid-1990s. Today, Angelenos following this trail, are rediscovering their own downtown and, through it, experiencing a reconnection to their City's destiny. They wonder how all of this could have happened when they weren't looking.

After World War II the historic core became a graveyard

The Tattooed Building: Victor Clothing Store on Broadway served recent immigrants from Mexico when they purchased their finery for special occasions. Ramiro Salcedo supported emerging Latino artists to paint the building inside and out.

Mayor Tom Bradley gave the Historic Core a reprieve by allowing jewelry manufacturing in the older office buildings of Broadway, Spring and Hill. Downtown became the second largest jewelry district in the country behind New York City.

Apparel manufacturing as well as jewelry manufacturing moved into the historic buildings after office towers were built on Bunker Hill.

Broadway – the place for film premieres and parades – until the rush to the suburbs and the advent of the neighborhood movie house.

In the early nineties, first Ira Yellin and then Tom Gilmore saw the value of restoring architectural and historic icons for a new era, creating adaptive reuse protocols that enabled residential and commercial revitalization.

Downtown has the largest collection of vintage
Beaux Arts, Spanish Revival and Art Deco buildings.

Before freeways and the flight to the suburbs, all roads led to downtown. The Subway Terminal Building on 4th and Hill as well as the Pacific Electric Building were as grand and welcoming to subway travelers as Union Station.

#1 Bunker Hill

Pacific Mutual Building

Fine Arts Building

Cicada at the Oviatt Building

Penthouse at the Oviatt Building

Biltmore Hotel

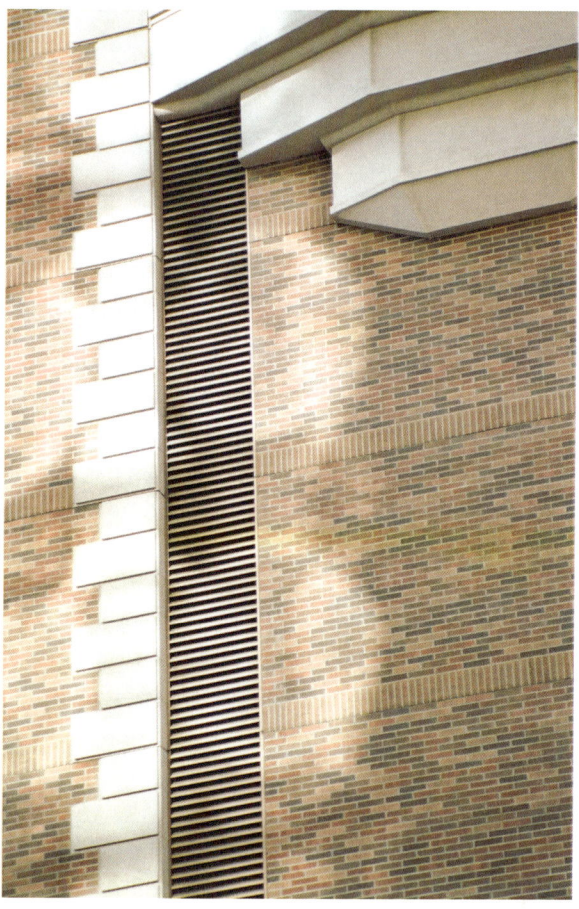

Bradbury Building

Street Art

Wall Art

Biddy Mason Courtyard

Bunker Hill Rising

CHINA CAFE
CHOP SUEY
CHOW MEIN
LACASA VERDE
PRODUCE

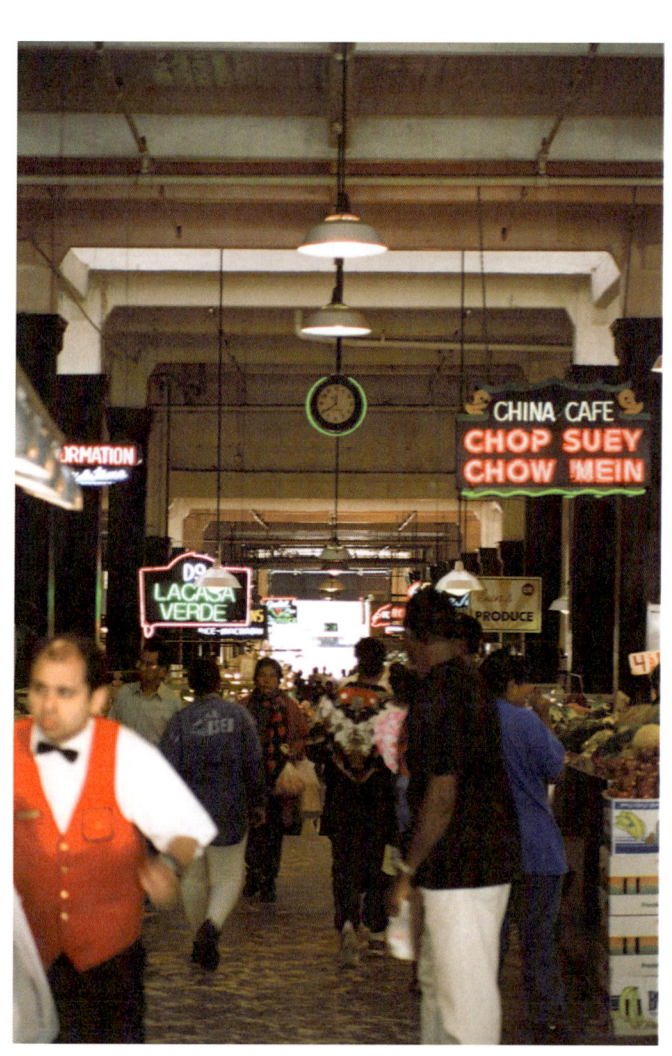

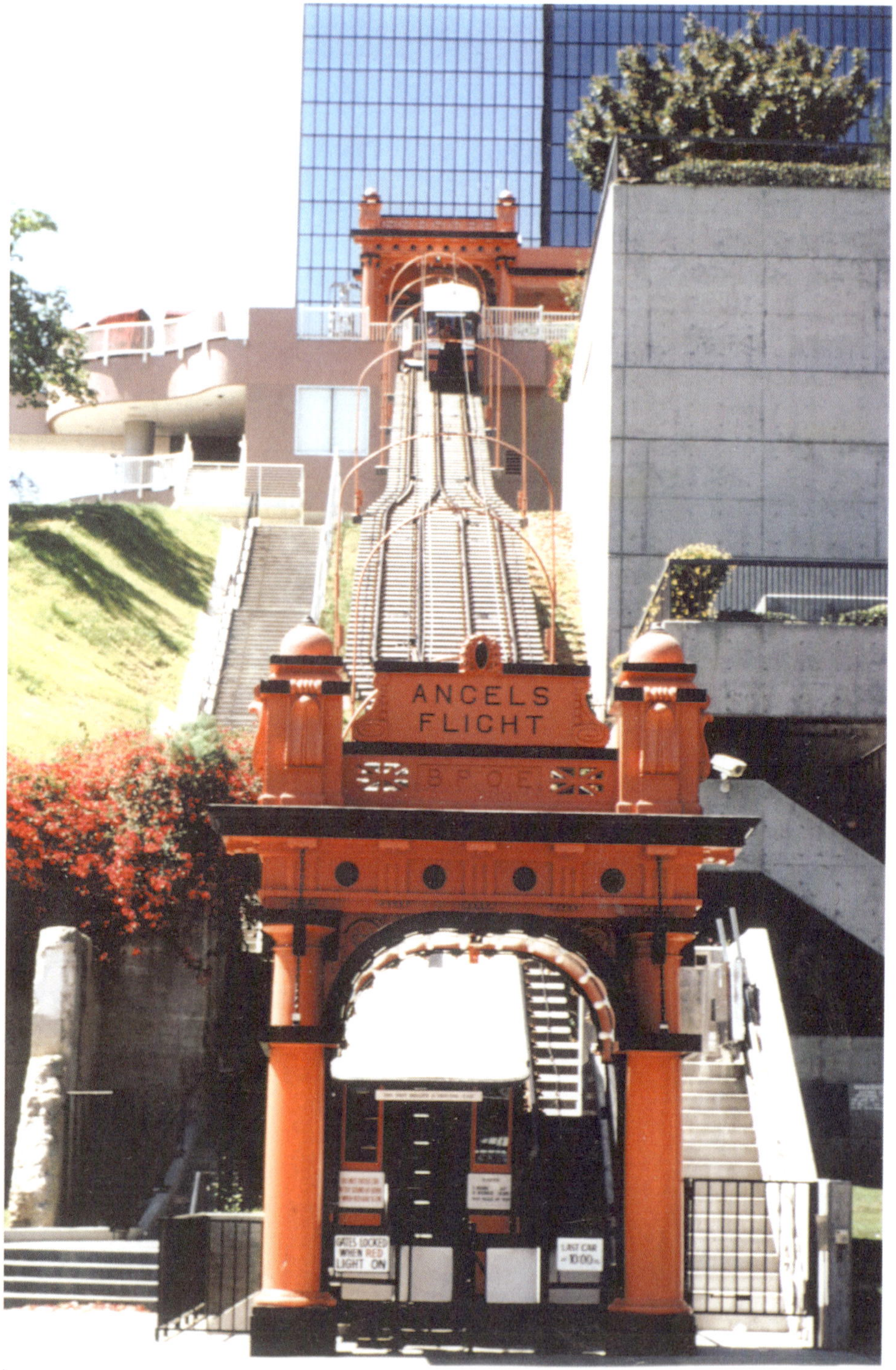
ANGELS FLIGHT
B P O E
GATES LOCKED WHEN RED LIGHT ON

Museum of Contemporary Art

About these Photographs

As a native Angeleno, I have always thought of LA as a perennial frontier, fertile ground for invention and entrepreneurship - a blank slate to rewrite early missteps in other places - a place for fresh starts, unfettered by the restraints of history, tradition and outdated obstacles. From the womb to the family, to the neighborhood to the larger Jewish community, my world expanded outward - not inward from the larger universe. Local history seemed irrelevant. I did not see that I belonged to the old City even though family members made their way through Boyle Heights; the Ellis Island of Los Angeles. But, periodically, my mother would take us downtown on the Venice streetcar to shop for housewares at the Broadway Department Store and clothes at the May Company with lunch in between at Clifton's Cafeteria. These were trips I did not cherish - overwhelmed by the crowds and fearful of the spooky prayer rooms at Clifton's.

In the 50s, returning vets from WWII spread out into the new suburbs and downtown lost its magnetism. Broadway's grand theaters no longer had an exclusive on premieres of Hollywood spectaculars, since small neighborhood theaters and drive-ins hosted simultaneous openings. Post-war LA did not need the escapist magic of downtown's magnificent theaters that had uplifted depression era and war era audiences. As Los Angeles had became the cutting edge of Modernism, the Art Deco, Spanish Revival and Gothic Revival buildings fell far behind the times.

In the 70s, Bunker Hill redevelopment swept aside Victorian mansions that had already slid into slum housing and declared the towers on the hill as the business center of the City. Mayor Tom Bradley and the Community Redevelopment Agency struggled to rescue the Historic Core by forcing government offices into depressingly obsolete buildings, encouraging low income housing, welcoming sweat shops serving the adjacent garment district, ignoring abuses of the signage ordinances on Broadway and turning a blind eye to the jewelry industry's environmental pollution in an effort to buy these buildings some time to be rediscovered.

Many years later, as the Arts community began to fill a void created by the social and economic retreat from the historic center of downtown, I had occasion to revisit these familiar downtown streets, now almost totally abandoned by mainstream businesses and customers. The old, familiar destinations were now patronized by Spanish-speaking shoppers and stores so totally out of synch with the grandeur of the buildings hosting them, that I had the impression I was witnessing a ghost town inhabited by a transient group of newcomers.

Yet, a few visionaries saw the inherent beauty, the intrinsic value and the untapped potential for downtown to be reborn as the much-needed soul of our City, with the power to draw together the vast diaspora Los Angeles had become and staked their lives on their vision. Ira Yellin was the first to act and rescued three iconic places on Broadway: the Bradbury Building (perhaps the most magical building in the Western world) as well as Grand Central Market and the Million Dollar Theater. Nick Patsaouras, a Greek immigrant who ventured here as a teenager, envisioned the key piece needed to link the City together - a public transportation network - that has, in fact, made all roads lead back to downtown. And Tom Gilmore invented a new LA life-style to accomplish the rebirth of long-vacant buildings: by sprucing up the historic buildings, going vertical, compressing living spaces for over-sprawled Angelenos and stimulating the density of amenities that make a neighborhood vibrant - almost overnight and single-handedly creating a new community of urban pioneers. After that, sensible business interests moved in and the rest is history, as they say.

I found myself watching all of this rebirthing swirling around me in the mid-1990s and got caught up with it. What was happening was so clear to me that, as an artist, it was not necessary for me to "translate" an imagined future vision via artistic techniques. I just clicked on what I saw and here it is.

Sandy Bleifer, 2014

Sandy Bleifer

my mother Rozella, sister Robie, brother Jerry and me at Clifton's on Broadway - September 11, 1951

www.ingramcontent.com/pod-product-compliance
Lightning Source LLC
Chambersburg PA
CBRC101356070526
44584CB00011B/340